The Impawsibly Good Book of CAT JOKES

The Impawsibly Good Book of CAT JOKES

165 Hissterical Jokes for Your Amewsment

Edited by Thomas Nowak

Illustrated by Nat Ellis

CHRONICLE BOOKS
SAN FRANCISCO

Copyright © 2025 by Maria Ribas Literary, LLC.
All rights reserved. No part of this book may be reproduced in any
form without written permission from the publisher.

Library of Congress Cataloging-in-Publication Data

Names: Nowak, Thomas, editor. | Ellis, Nat, illustrator.
Title: The impawsibly good book of cat jokes :
165 hissterical jokes for your amewsment /
edited by Thomas Nowak ; illustrated by Nat Ellis.
Other titles: Book of cat jokes
Description: San Francisco : Chronicle Books, [2025]
Identifiers: LCCN 2024052701 | ISBN 9781797232522 (hardcover)
Subjects: LCSH: Cats--Humor. | American wit and humor.
Classification: LCC PN6231.C23 I47 2025 |
DDC 808.8/03629752--dc23/eng/20250125
LC record available at https://lccn.loc.gov/2024052701

Manufactured in China.

Design by Maggie Edelman.
Illustrations by Nat Ellis.

10 9 8 7 6 5 4 3 2 1

Chronicle books and gifts are available at special quantity
discounts to corporations, professional associations,
literacy programs, and other organizations. For details and
discount information, please contact our premiums department
at corporategifts@chroniclebooks.com or at 1-800-759-0190.

Chronicle Books LLC
680 Second Street
San Francisco, California 94107
www.chroniclebooks.com

FOR THE CAT LADIES

What kind of kitten do you want with you in an extreme climate?

A SURVIVAL KIT.

What does a cat like to eat on a hot day?

A MICECREAM CONE.

How many cats can sit in an empty box?

ONLY ONE. AFTER THAT, THE BOX ISN'T EMPTY.

Why did the kitty get an A on her English assignment?

SHE PROPERLY USED AN INDEPENDENT CLAWS.

Have you heard about the cat who had his membership revoked?

HE HAD FORGOTTEN TO PAY HIS ANNUAL FLEAS.

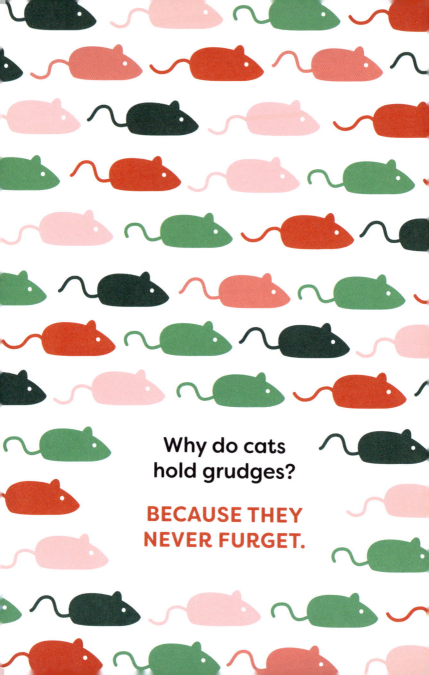

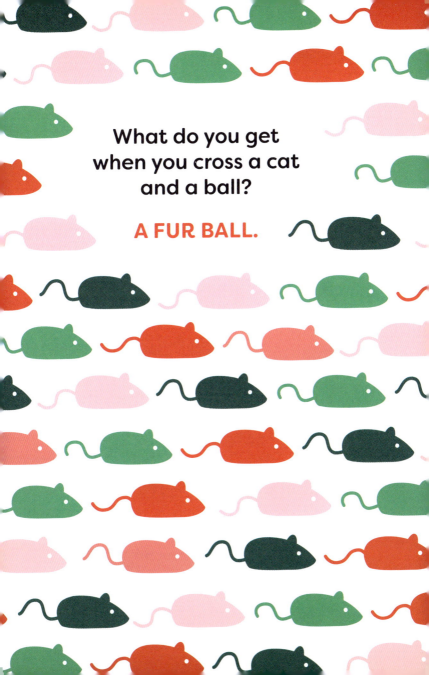

What do you get when you cross a cat and a ball?

A FUR BALL.

How do you hire a cat?

PUT UP A LADDER.

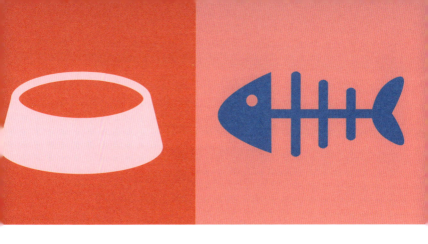

Who is a kitten's favorite singer?

KITTY PURRY.

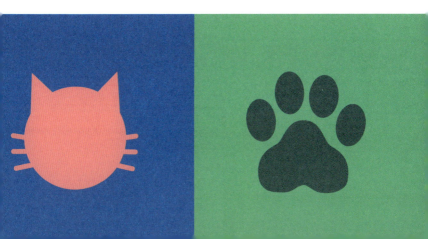

What did the teacher say after he caught the kitten cheating?

"DON'T BE A COPYCAT."

What do you call a fussy cat?

PURRSNICKETY.

What do you call a fibbing cat?

LION.

What sports do cats play?

HAIRBALL!

What did the alien say to the cat?

"TAKE ME TO YOUR LITTER."

What do cats wear to bed?

PAWJAMAS.

What is smarter than a talking cat?

NOTHING—OR AT LEAST THAT'S WHAT MY CAT TOLD ME.

What do you get when you cross a snow leopard with a snowman?

FROSTBITE.

KNOCK, KNOCK.

Who's there?

IVAN.

Ivan who?

IVAN CHECKING MY BOWL OVER AND OVER, AND IT'S STILL EMPTY.

Did you hear about the cat who burned dinner?

SHE HAD TO START OVER FROM SCRATCH.

Did you hear about the angry cat?

HE GOT HOT UNDER THE COLLAR.

What kind of cat does Luke Skywalker have?

A LIGHTSABER-TOOTHED CAT.

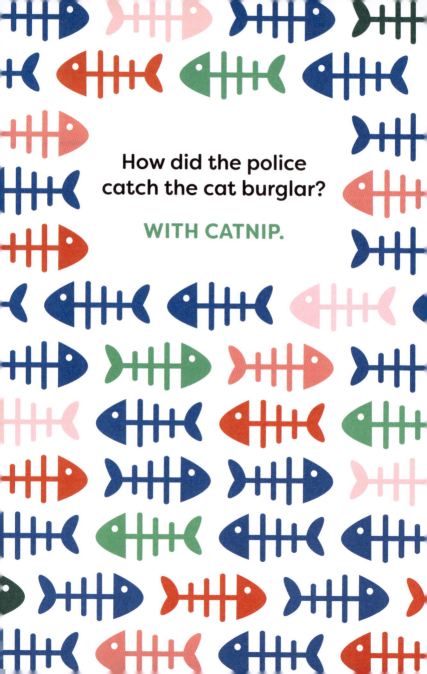

How did the police catch the cat burglar?

WITH CATNIP.

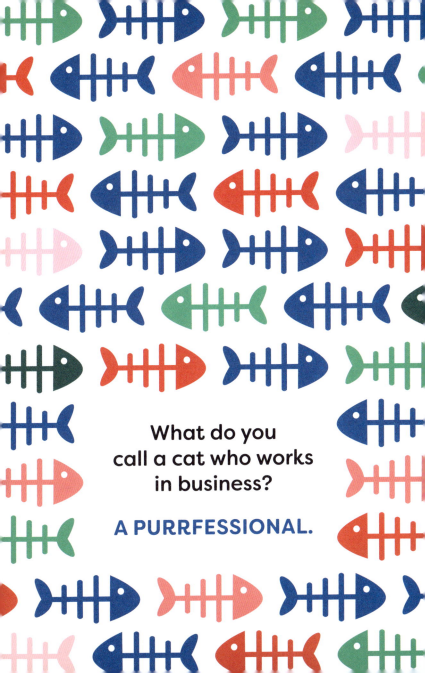

KNOCK, KNOCK.

Who's there?

FELINE.

Feline who?

FELINE FINE AFTER MY FIFTH NAP OF THE DAY!

Why did the cat slouch?

HE HAD BAD PAWSTURE.

My cat hates to work.

SHE ONLY DOES THE BARE MEWNIMUM.

What do you call
a kitten who cuts her
hair really short?

A BOBCAT!

If a cat loses her tail, where does she go?

THE RETAIL STORE.

What's a cat's favorite flower?

A TIGER LILY.

What did the lion say when the gazelle jumped on his back?

"LUNCH IS ON ME TODAY!"

What did the party-animal kitten say?

"TURN UP THE MEWSIC AND GET THIS PAWTY STARTED!"

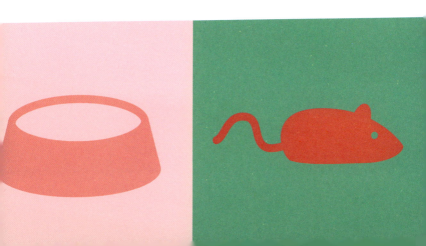

Why did the cat avoid eating lemons?

THEY MADE HIM A SOURPUSS.

What party game do kittens love to play?

MEWSICAL CHAIRS.

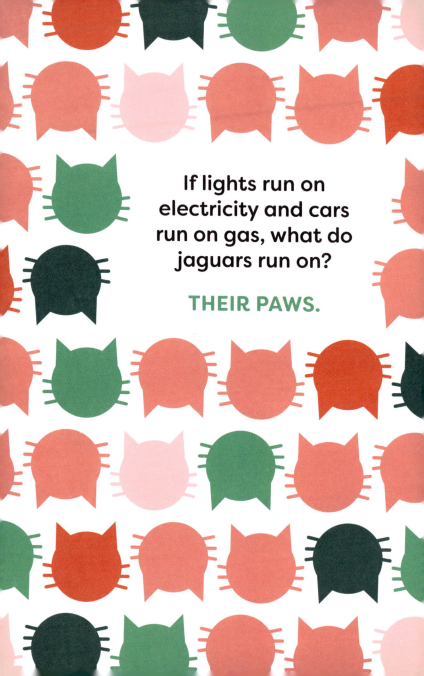

If lights run on electricity and cars run on gas, what do jaguars run on?

THEIR PAWS.

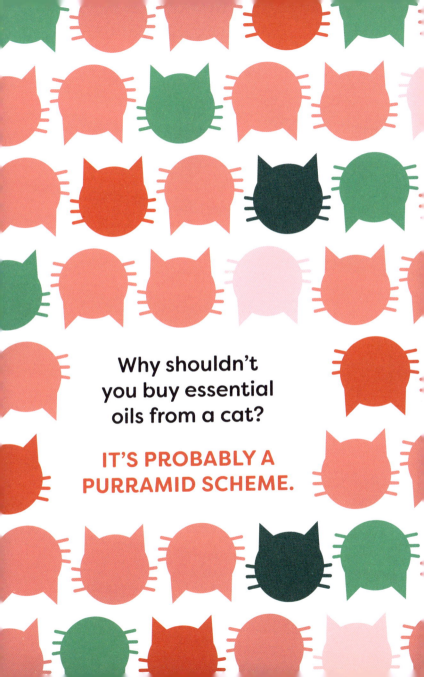

Why did the kitten have so many library fines?

BECAUSE HE KEPT THE BOOKS OUT FUREVER.

What does a cat look for
in a neighborhood?

**A MICE FAMILY NEXT
DOOR SHE CAN INVITE
OVER FOR DINNER.**

What is a cat's least
favorite jacket?

A FLEAS-LINED COAT.

What is a kitten's favorite nursery rhyme?

"THREE BLIND MICE."

What is a
kitten's favorite kind
of sticker?

SCRATCH-AND-SNIFF.

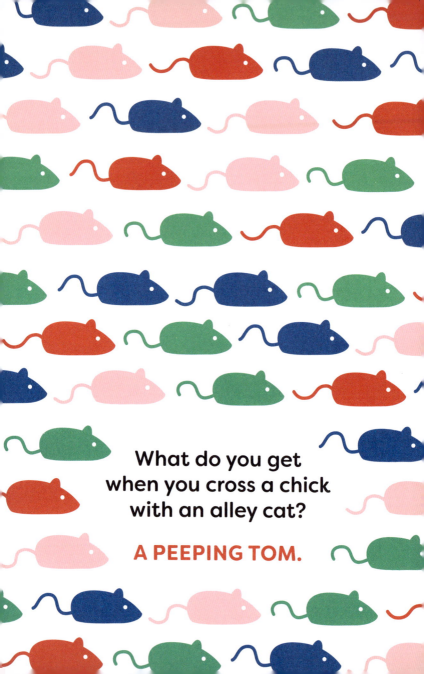

What do you get when you cross a chick with an alley cat?

A PEEPING TOM.

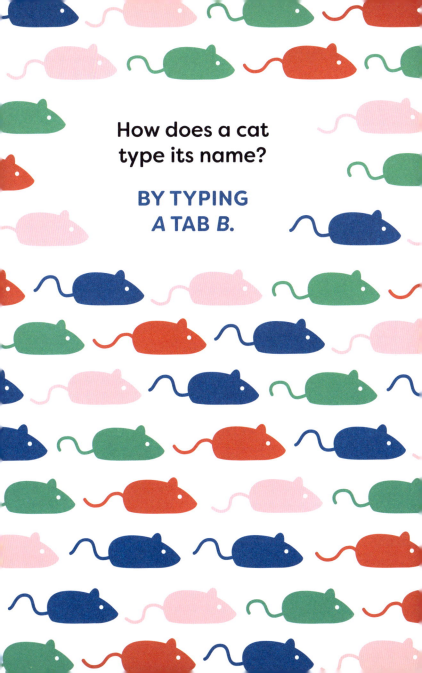

How does a cat type its name?

BY TYPING *A TAB B.*

Why do cats look down on dogs?

THEY KNOW ALL DOGS ARE INFURIOR TO THEM!

KNOCK, KNOCK.

Who's there?

PASTURE.

Pasture who?

PASTURE LEG AND HAD TO RUB AGAINST IT.

KNOCK, KNOCK.

Who's there?

VENICE.

Venice who?

VENICE IT NAP TIME AROUND HERE?

What does a cat
call a mouse?

DELICIOUS.

What do polite cats say?

"HAVE A MICE DAY!"

Why did the cat go to a therapist?

SHE HAD CLAWSTROPHOBIA.

Why is it so hard for a leopard to hide?

BECAUSE HE'S ALWAYS SPOTTED.

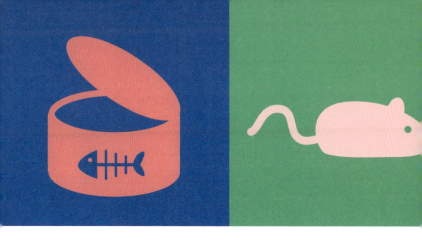

What do cat artists usually paint?

SELF-PAWTRAITS.

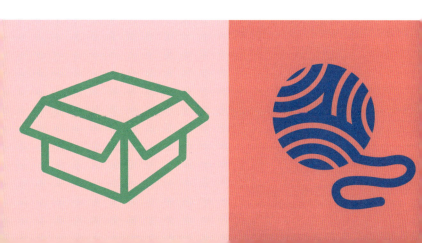

Why do cats always beat dogs in video games?

THEY HAVE NINE LIVES.

Why did the cat get a dog?

WELL, SHE WASN'T GOING TO FETCH HER OWN PAPER, WAS SHE?

Where do tigers exercise?

THE JUNGLE GYM.

Why couldn't the cat use his credit card to buy a 99¢ can of cat food?

THE STORE HAD A MEOWNIMUM PURRCHASE POLICY.

What did the cat's therapist say?

"PAWSE BEFORE REACTING."

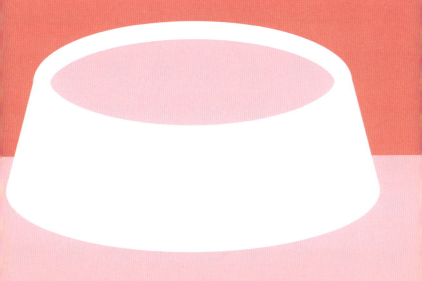

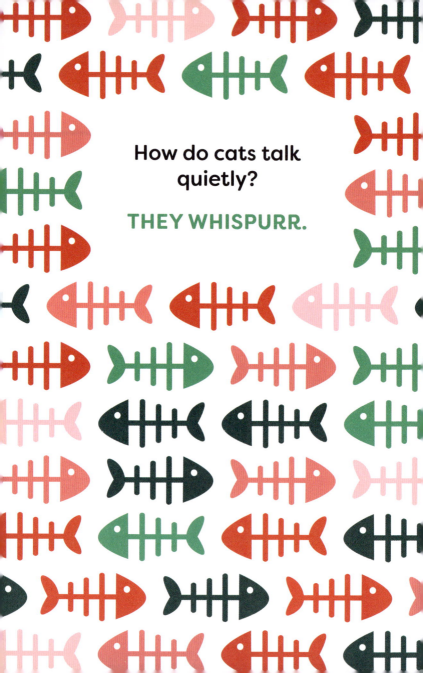

How do cats talk quietly?

THEY WHISPURR.

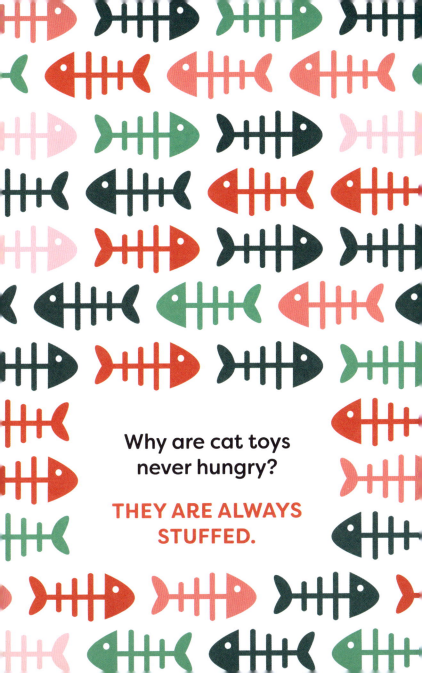

What do cats like to eat for breakfast?

MICE KRISPIES.

What does a cat say when she really can't do something?

"I LITTER-ALLY CAN'T!"

What does a cat drink during the summer?

MICE TEA.

Why do kittens go to medical school?

TO BECOME FIRST AID KITS.

KNOCK, KNOCK.

Who's there?

ANNIE.

Annie who?

IS ANNIE-BODY GOING TO FEED ME OR WHAT?!

Why don't cats
like online shopping?

**THEY PREFER
CAT-ALOGS.**

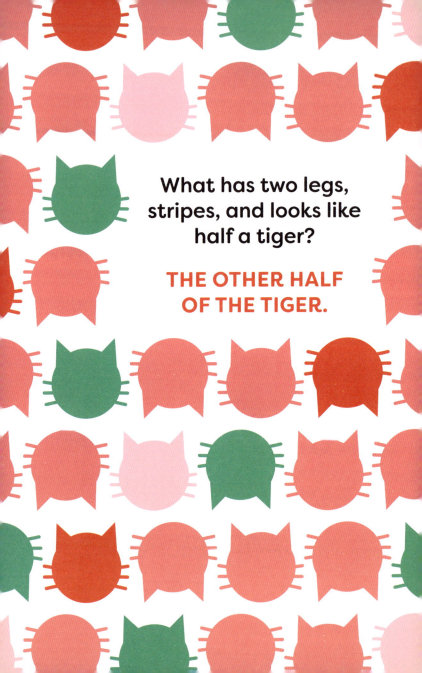

What has two legs, stripes, and looks like half a tiger?

THE OTHER HALF OF THE TIGER.

If a human with two legs is a biped, what's a tiger with four legs?

A STRI-PED.

What's a cat's favorite book?

HAIRY PAWTER AND THE GOBLET OF CAT TREATS.

What's a cat's favorite song?

"FUR ELISE."

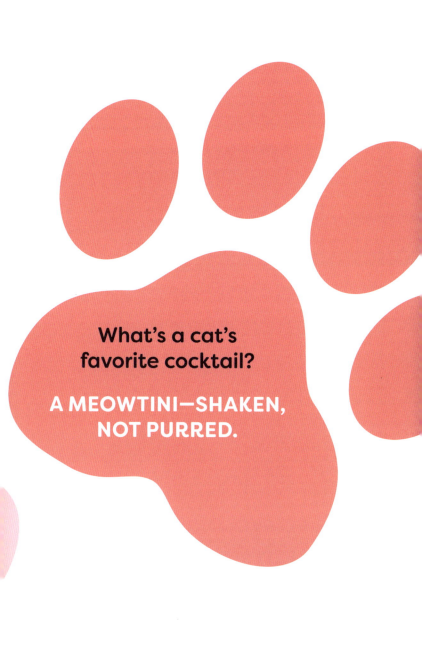

What's the best cat joke?

CAT THINK OF ANY RIGHT MEOW.

My cat told a joke today, but I didn't laugh.

HE TOOK IT PURRSONALY.

What did the cat say when asked to help out around the house?

"NAH, I'M NOT FELINE IT."

What did the kitten say when she was turned away from the margarita bar for being underage?

"YOU HAVE GATO BE KITTEN ME."

Why did the cat wear a tuxedo?

HE WAS FELINE FANCY!

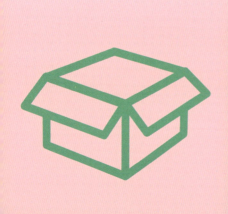

How do you know your cat has been in your office?

YOUR MOUSE HAS TEETH MARKS ON IT.

Why didn't the cat get promoted to management?

HE HAD TERRIBLE LITTERSHIP SKILLS.

What did the lions say when they saw an elephant?

"OH, THERE'S THE BUFFET!"

Where did the cat go for culture?

THE MEWSEUM.

Why did the kitten nibble on a lampshade?

HE WANTED A LIGHT SNACK.

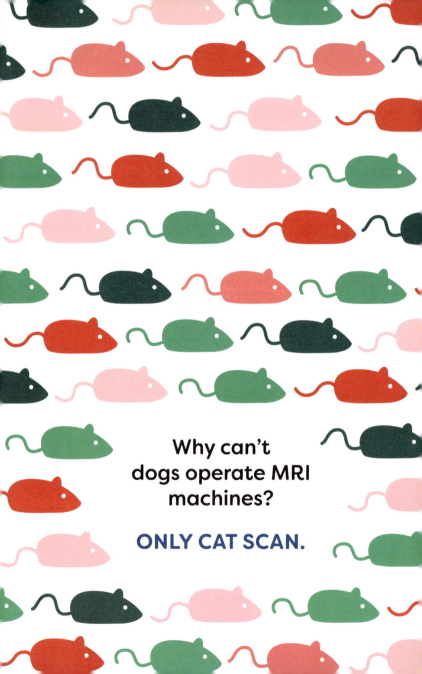

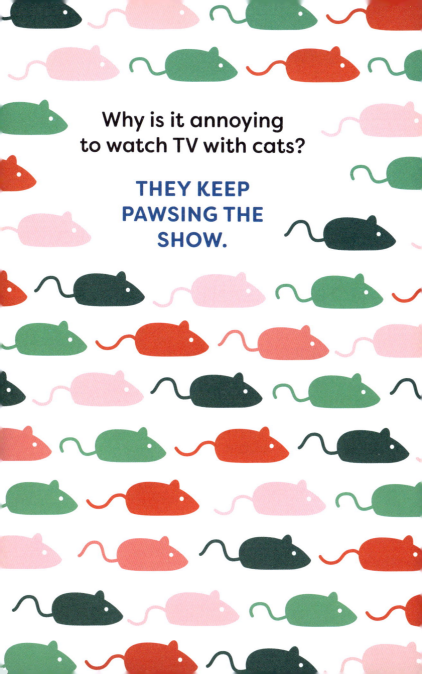

KNOCK, KNOCK.

Who's there?

JUNEAU.

Juneau who?

JUNEAU A GOOD SPOT FOR A CATNAP?

Why are cats good at keeping secrets?

THEY DON'T HISS AND TAIL.

Which side of an ocelot has the most spots?

THE OUTSIDE.

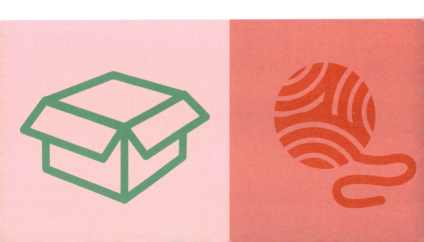

How is a cat like a coin?

THEY HAVE A HEAD ON ONE SIDE AND A TAIL ON THE OTHER.

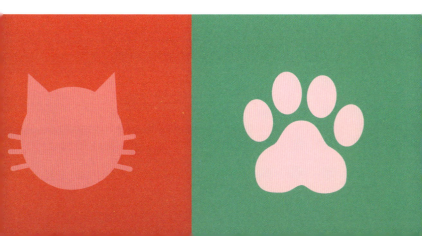

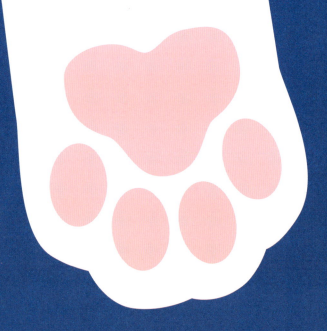

Where is one place that your cat can sit but you can't?

YOUR LAP.

What kind of jewelry do fancy cats wear?

PURRL NECKLACES.

What is a cat's favorite type of fashion?

HAUTE CATURE.

I have a pencil that was once owned by Shake-speare. But, thanks to the kitten, it's so chewed up I can't tell if it's 2B or not 2B.

What did the cat say when asked to go to work?

"WHISKER ME BACK TO BED!"

What steps do you take if a cougar is chasing you?

BIG ONES!

Why is your cat such a snob?

SHE'S AN ARISTOCAT!

What do you call
a stylish cat?

A DANDY LION.

Why did the cat complain all the time?

HE HEARD THAT CATS HAVE WHINE LIVES!

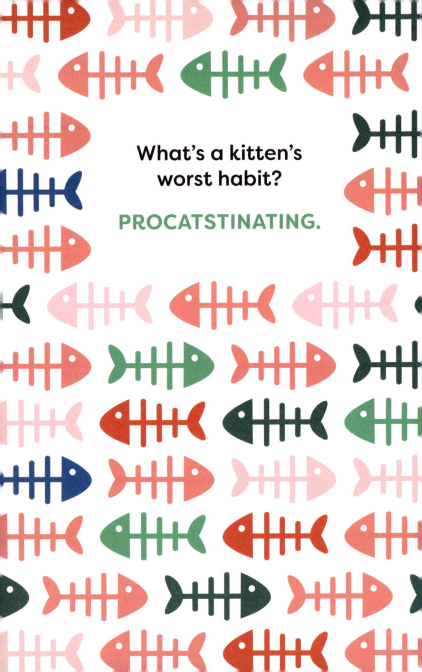

What's a kitten's worst habit?

PROCATSTINATING.

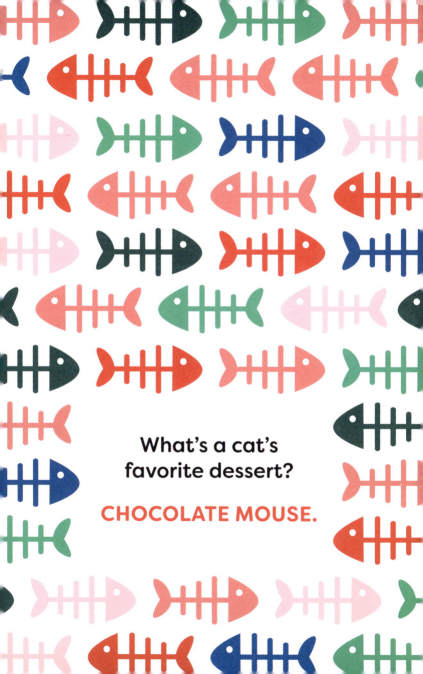

Why is the cat scared to look under the bed?

BECAUSE OF THE MEOWNSTER!

Why can't cats get together to play cards?

THERE ARE TOO MANY CHEETAHS.

What do you call a kitten with eight legs?

AN OCTOPUSS.

How does a lion greet a gazelle?

"PLEASED TO EAT YOU!"

Why did the cat get pulled over by the police?

BECAUSE HE LITTERED.

KNOCK, KNOCK.

Who's there?

EDEN.

Eden who?

EDEN SOME CATNIP—YOU WANT IN?

What do you call
a cat who is always
telling on you?

A TATTLETAIL.

What game do kittens play with their friends?

FOLLOW THE LASER.

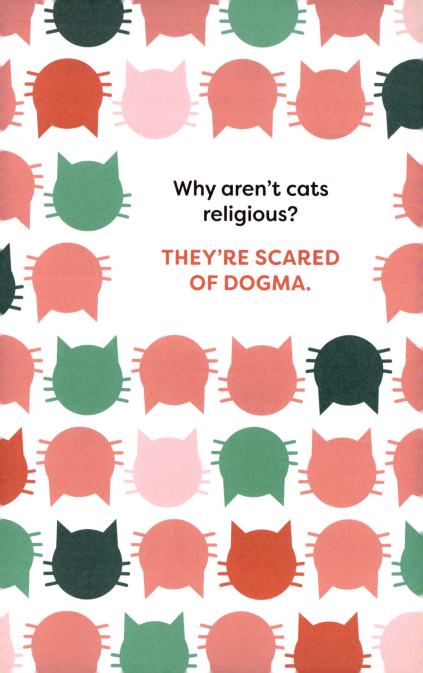

Why aren't cats religious?

THEY'RE SCARED OF DOGMA.

Why are there so many unsolved mysteries in the forest?

TOO MANY MISSING LYNX.

Why don't kittens play fetch?

THEY'D RATHER CAT-CH A NAP.

What did the cat say when asked to do chores?

"STOP STRESSING MEOWT."

What's a kitten's favorite band?

MEW KIDS ON THE BLOCK.

Why did the cougar eat a gymnast?

THE VET PUT HIM ON A BALANCED DIET.

Why does the cat do stand-up?

HE LIVES FOR THE APAWS.

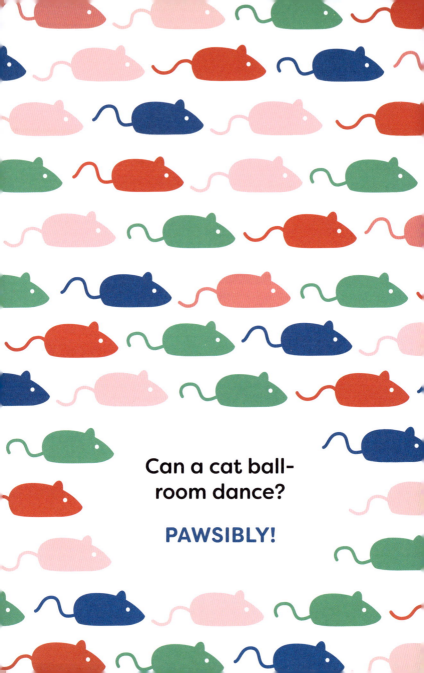

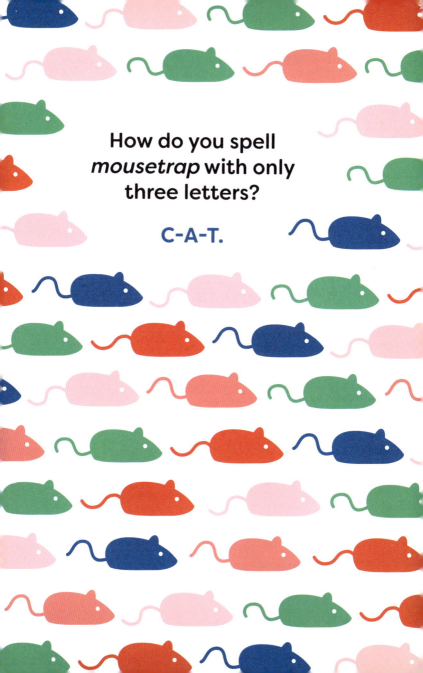

How do you spell *mousetrap* with only three letters?

C-A-T.

Did you hear
about the cat who ate
a bad sausage?

IT WAS THE WURST.

Why was the cat so small?

BECAUSE SHE ONLY DRANK CONDENSED MILK!

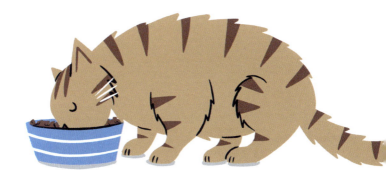

What did the motivational poster at the cat's office say?

"WITH THE RIGHT CATTITUDE, ANYTHING IS PAWSIBLE!"

Did you hear about the passenger who had to be escorted off the airplane?

SHE LET THE CAT OUT OF THE BAG.

Why do cats love coffee?

IT MAKES THEM PURRKY.

What is a cat's favorite type of exercise?

PAWLATES!

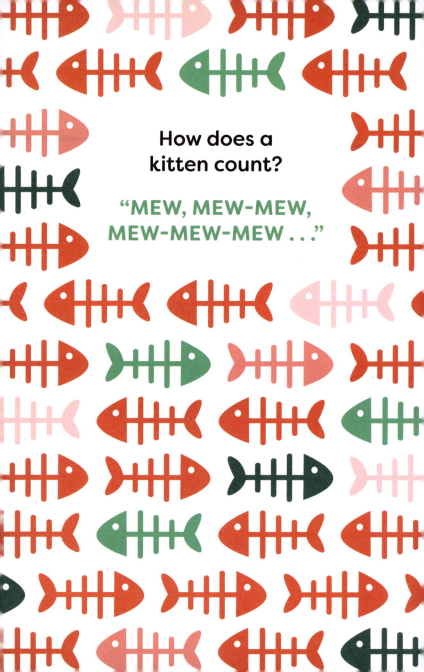

How does a kitten count?

"MEW, MEW-MEW, MEW-MEW-MEW..."

Why are cats so confident?

THEY KNOW THEY'RE PURRTY.

What kind of cars do cats prefer to drive?

FURARRIS.

Did you hear about the cat who lost his left legs?

HE'S ALL RIGHT NOW.

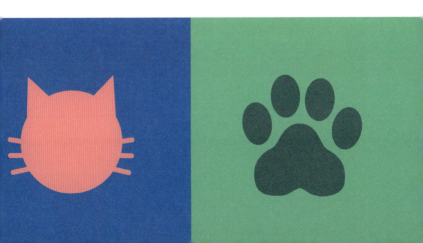

Why are cats better than toads?

CATS HAVE NINE LIVES, AND TOADS CROAK EVERY NIGHT.

Why do cats make good comedians?

THEY'RE HISSTERICAL.

Who gives kittens
the best presents?

SANTA CLAWS!

Which bird did the cat eat?

A SWALLOW.

What did the cat order at the coffee shop?

A CATPUCCINO.

What did the
cat say when she
stubbed her toe?

"MEOWCH!"

What did the cat say when reading this book?

"THESE PUNS ARE APAWLING."

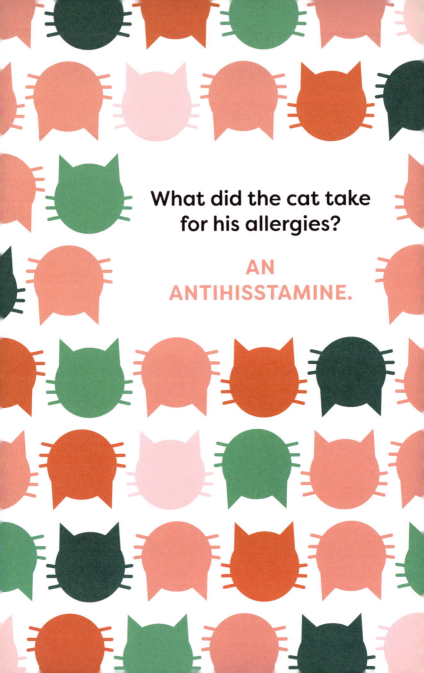

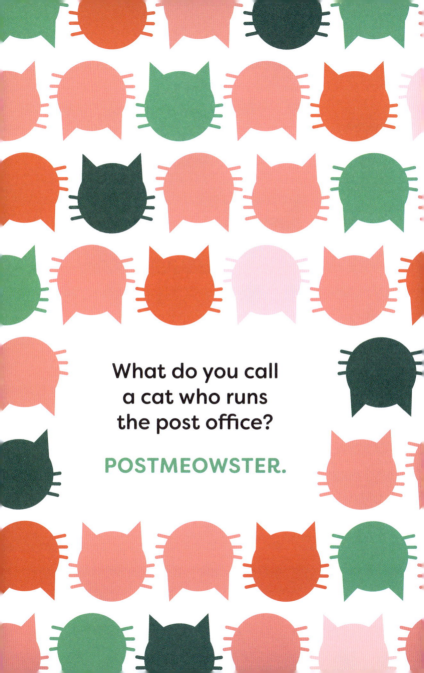

Did you hear about
the cat who drank
five bowls of water?

**HE SET A NEW LAP
RECORD.**

How did the kitten feel about
the horror movie?

**IT WAS COMPLETELY
HAIR-RAISING.**

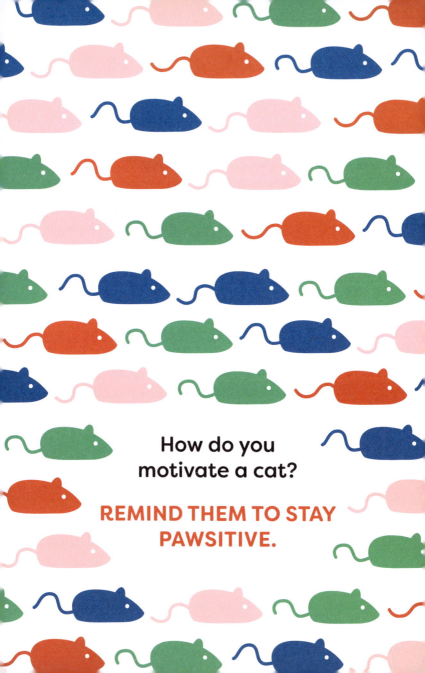

If optimists see a glass half full and pessimists see a glass half empty, what do cat owners see?

A GLASS KNOCKED OVER.

What's a cat's favorite TV show?

DOWNTON TABBY.

Why did the kitten do so well on the test?

IT WAS HISSTORY.

What do you call a cat who has two ears?

IT DOESN'T MATTER. CATS DON'T USUALLY COME WHEN CALLED.

Why do kittens love to read the news?

SO MANY CAT-ASTROPHES!

Have you ever seen a catfish?

NO. HOW WOULD THEY HOLD THE ROD AND REEL?

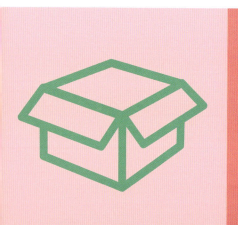

Why did the kitten get sent to the principal's office?

HE HAD A BAD CATTITUDE IN CLASS.

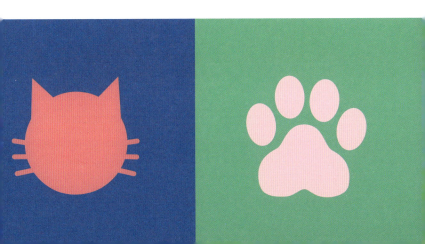

What happens when you cross a lion with a watchdog?

THE MAILPERSON STOPS DELIVERING YOUR MAIL.

What do you call a cat who won't sink in water?

A BOBCAT.

If puppies make a
dog pile, what do
kittens make?

A MEOWTAIN.

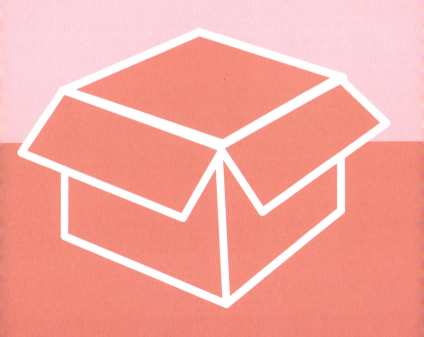

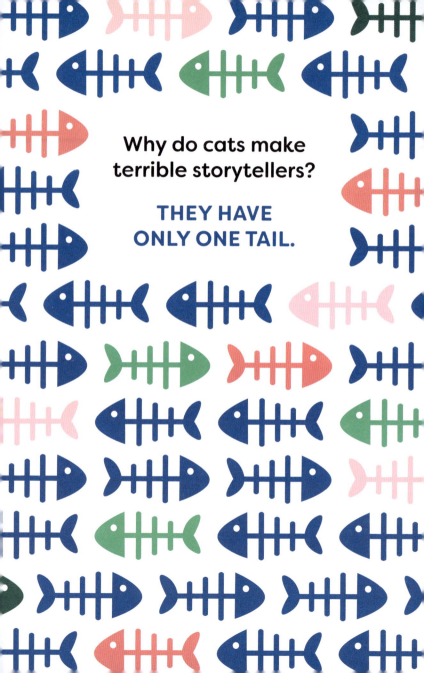

Why do cats make terrible storytellers?

THEY HAVE ONLY ONE TAIL.

What does a kitten call her dad's dad?

GRANDPAW.

What has black, white, and orange stripes?

A TABBY RIDING A ZEBRA.

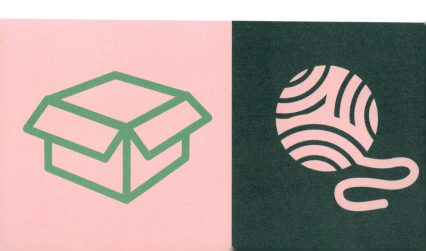

Why did the cat become a comedian?

SHE HAD LOTS OF CAT-CHY JOKES.

What did the kitten have at her birthday party?

A POUNCE HOUSE.

What does knowing a cat feel like?

PURR JOY.

Why was the cat so agitated?

HE WAS IN A BAD MEWD.

What do you call a cat in a turtleneck?

STUCK.

What did the tiger yell when he jumped into the swimming pool?

"FURBALL!"

Why did the kitten like water?

SHE WAS A MEWMAID.

What do you call
a cat with a
criminal record?

A PURRPETRATOR.

KNOCK, KNOCK.

Who's there?

TAMARA.

Tamara who?

TAMARA I WANT TUNA FOR DINNER.

What does the lion say to his friends before they go out hunting for food?

"LET US PREY."

Why did the cat scratch bedposts but not chairs?

BECAUSE THE CHAIR WAS ARMED.

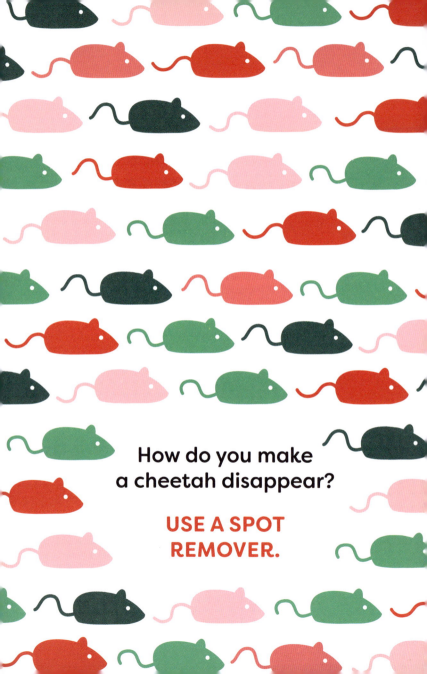

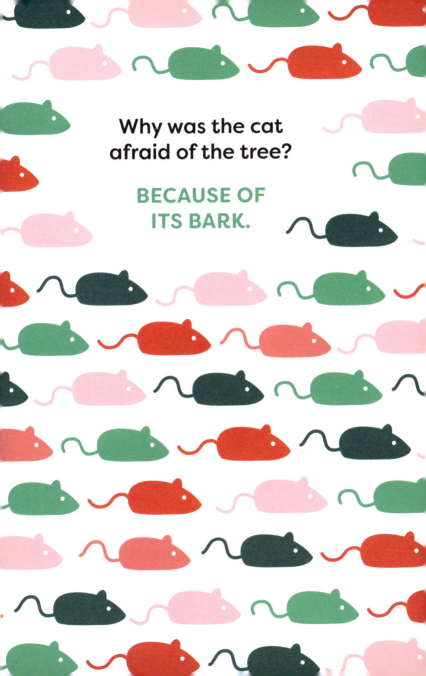

THANK YOU to the cats everywhere who endure our bad jokes, snort-chortles, and alarming degree of love for them. We do it all for you. ALL OF IT.

Thank you to Maria Ribas at Stonesong for her ceaseless belief and really quite excessive enthusiasm for this project (and for bringing the cackles at every single joke).

An extra big thank you to Olivia Roberts, who got this book from the very first meow and could not have been a better cat editor and cat lady to shape this cutie of a book.

Kibble must be given to Nat Ellis of Nat Ellis Illustration for the irresistible kitty illustrations that bring this book to life. And thank you to Maggie Edelman for the playful and pawtastic design.

Thank you to the entire team of cat people at Chronicle Books, whose talent and thoughtfulness have made this book much more than the sum of its jokes.